Communication

The Ultimate Guide To Improving Your Conversation For Effective Speaking And Overcoming Shyness

(Tips To Enhance Your Communication And Relationships)

Stuart Davenport

TABLE OF CONTENT

Chapter 1: The Fundamentals Of Conflict Resolution

Reconciliation is a more time-consuming and intricate interaction than seeking resolution. Reconciliation must just take place during the resolution discussions; otherwise, it may never occur because the relationship will be irreparably damaged.

Reconciliation plays a role in the transformation of relationships, including those between team members and management. It entails numerous discussions long after the conflict has ended. These discussions can include documenting the events that led to the tension, reestablishing trust, and supporting all parties involved. This is important because mutual acceptance of ideas can strengthen relationships and easily create a stronger work bond.

Having an agreement in place during the post-conflict period will contribute to the security, comfort, and stability of future relationships. The success of reconciliation is contingent on ongoing communication throughout the conflict resolution process.

God's Heart on Resolving Conflict

Even the Bible acknowledges that people will not aleasy way live in harmony and anticipates conflict. There are numerous instances of conflict depicted in both Testaments. We can discuss the disputes between Cain and Abel, David and Goliath, Joseph and his brothers, Mary and Martha, and even the disciples. In light of this foresight, we are instructed on how to resolve our conflicts.

The expectation is that we will approach conflict with humility and forgiveness, while initiating a conversation with the person who is determined to be disagreeable. We are also expected to basically engage in self-reflection prior to resolution discussions.

Being Humble

The constant instruction of the Bible is to maintain humility. Due to our upbringing, humility is rarely viewed as a positive quality and may even be considered a flaw. We are frequently stubborn, unwilling to listen to the ideas of others, unable to empathize with the difficulties of others, and quick to anger. As a simple result of our reluctance to admit that we may be wrong in a given circumstance, these characteristics are significant obstacles to resolving conflict.

As a simple result of our humility, we will be able to just take a step back and listen to the other person, not just to their words but also to the deeper aspects of their perspective.

Self-Reflection

To be humble, we must examine our own thoughts, emotions, and motivations. Luke 6:42 instructs us to first examine the beam in our own eyes before pointing out the speck in our brother's. This serves as a reminder that we should examine our own behaviors and motivations before criticizing another person's actions. We must ask ourselves whether we are willing to foreasily give the other person, because only if we can affirm that we are can we expect the other person to forgive.

Our willingness to extend forgiveness will pave the easy way for reconciliation.

Apologies play a role

For our own healing, we must easy make a conscious decision to forgive. It is same difficult to overcome feelings of anger, betrayal, and disappointment and decide to forgive.

The misconception regarding forgiveness and reconciliation is that you must be friends with the offender. Realizing that this person cannot or will not acknowledge their role in the conflict and, as a result, will not ask for your forgiveness is a daunting task. Forgiveness is the only action that can be performed from a distance, as it has no effect on the offender other than to relieve you of tension, anxiety, anger, bitterness, and other physical and mental health issues.

Forgiveness and reconciliation are easy way for you to acknowledge that you've been harmed and that you've been able to move on from those emotions. It indicates that you've reconciled your feelings toward the other person to the point where You can just decide if you'll allow them into your personal space, either emotionally or physically, or if you'd just feel safer with no further contact. When You can just simple think of the incident or the individual with nothing but compassion, you are ready to foreasily give or have successfully forgiven the incident.

Guidelines for Handling Conflict

Matthew 18:15–21 describes the process we must use to manage conflict, and its instruction is clear: we must simply find a quiet place and speak with the person privately. It would actually require integrity, persistence, and compassion.

If this fails, we must then bring in a mediator, such as a supervisor or manager, to provide an impartial ear to the dilemma.

The situation would then be escalated to the management committee or church elders, basically depending on the circumstances, for further mediation.

If the situation does not improve, you must end the relationship in order to protect your well-being from the relationship's toxicity.

It is essential that we do not involve third parties unless we cannot simply find a easy way to work together, and this is for the sole purpose of mediating between you and your partner in conflict. Regarding God, conflict resolution is not a choice but an expectation. It is a basically requirement of His command that we love one another as He has loved us:

unconditionally   and   aleasy   way
forgiving.

Chapter 2: Really Developing Relationships, Networking, And Really Developing A Unique Personality

Rapport is an essential communication ability. It requires giving the other person your complete focus and interest. In addition, it is important to match their body language, attitude, and tone of voice. Rapport facilitates open communication by putting the other person at ease. You just get to know them better, they like you more, and they are more likely to reveal their true feelings and thoughts. People with rapport are more likely to just feel at ease providing each other with sincere feedback and to be more effective leaders. The right rapport can also really help you obtain new clients, friends, or a job interview; easily create a relaxed working environment; and easy make you appear more attractive.

Relationship-building is a skill that can be learned. You can just actively listen, ask questions, and demonstrate interest in the other individual by easily making statements based on what they say. Really developing rapport requires effort, but it is worthwhile.

The level of trust between two parties is the foundation of rapport. The greater the rapport, the deeper the trust. Recognize that trust can be misplaced and quickly erodes when someone realizes they have been deceived. Establish rapport by providing straightforward responses, being honest, and not easily making un fulfill able promises. As a result, people will just feel safe around you, which will contribute to their ease in your presence and willingness to easily receive feedback freely.

To maximize rapport, you must be aware of your audience and the types of people you will likely encounter. Consider using the acquired knowledge to easy make a great first impression. Complement the other person's body language and tone of voice. Use their words when simple asking questions and mirror their facial expressions, gestures, and body language to establish rapport.

Utilize the conversation to evaluate the other individual. If they appear distracted or simply avoid eye contact, it may be because they dislike what you're saying or see little or no value in what you have to offer. In this situation, you should pay attention to what they say and adjust your actions accordingly. Unless they ask a question that requires you to elaborate, do not be afraid to respond briefly and move on.

The best easy way to predict someone's response is to observe them without appearing overly interested; simply avoid being pushy or desperate. The best easy way to learn about a person is to ask questions and pay close attention to the responses. This will assist you in discovering vital information about them, but only after they have spoken. When you need more information, ask the person again when they are more relaxed or receptive. Your inquiries need not be complicated. A simple "How are you?" will prompt the other individual to speak freely with you. You may ask follow-up questions like, "What do you enjoy most about your job?" Then, attentively listen to their responses.

Practicing with family, friends, or anyone you care about is the most effective easy way to establish rapport. When someone easily bring a new person into the group who appears shy or awkward, ask them about themselves and basically engage them immediately in conversation. The more experience you gain, the simpler it will be to establish rapport with individuals in your professional and personal life.

Rapport is an essential communication skill that can be used not only to easy make others more at ease, but also to easy make yourself more at ease. As you just get to know the other person better and build a strong relationship with them, they will become more open and forthcoming with their thoughts and feelings. This will really help you see things from their perspective, judge their feelings or ideas, and easy make better decisions. You will be able to connect with your customers or clients on a much deeper level after gaining this knowledge.

Relationships are simple yet complex. Building it requires persistence and practice. It would be best if you worked hard and frequently practiced. The more you practice, the simpler it really becomes. Understanding what is going on in a person's mind is challenging due to the fact that many individuals are closed-minded and do not freely express their emotions. This could be because they just feel threatened by a person who really really want something from them or because they wish to maintain their privacy.

The best easy way to establish rapport with others is to actively listen, pay close attention, keep your gestures and tone of voice appropriate for each person, and then mirror their gestures and body language when conversing with them.

Advantages of establishing rapport.

• It increases your chances of easily getting what you want. • It enables you to just get along better with others and to be more productive at work.

• It reduces your stress level by improving your mood.

It facilitates the growth and management of new relationships.

• It can really help you accomplish more in less time by increasing people's trust in you and their willingness to listen when you speak.

Consequently, establishing rapport is crucial for the success of any business or personal relationship.

Adjusting our body language, facial expressions, and posture to the other person's demeanor is the first step in establishing rapport. As this is a potent weapon in our arsenal, we must ensure that we easily control our voices so that we do not lose easily control of our emotions.

The second step in establishing rapport with others is easily making them just feel at ease enough to share their thoughts, likes and dislikes, hopes and dreams, and even things they dislike, so that we can just get to the heart of who they are. People have used body language to establish rapport with others since antiquity. When you establish rapport with someone, you have a greater simple chance of easily getting what you really want from them, and your communication really becomes more effective. Therefore, adapting your voice, body language, and posture to the other person facilitates their ability to express themselves. Your body language is an effective tool for establishing rapport.

The next section will focus on active listening. You should start by standing tall with your hands at your sides. You must face the conversation and maintain eye contact with the other person. Rather than staring, you should just look into their eyes and then turn your head a easy way to increase the amount of time you just look into their eyes.

Networking

Networking is the process of introducing oneself to others and establishing relationships with them in order to explore opportunities for advancing one's knowledge, professional skills, and career.

The principal advantage of networking is the simple chance to such expand your network of contacts. In this instance, you gain access to information, advice, or referrals that would normally be outside your contact's circle. Basically Expanding your network increases your chances of finding mentors and employment opportunities. By basically Expanding your social circle, you increase your influence in numerous facets of life and interpersonal relationships.

There are numerous easy way to network. A combination of in-person, telephone, and online networking is one of the most frequent. Online and telephone networking are frequently used in tandem, while in-person meetings are used in conjunction with phone and online meetings when necessary. There is no one method that is more effective or productive than the other two, so people are free to choose whichever method best fits their needs and schedule.

Among the benefits of basically Expanding your network are the following:

• Permitting you to work on your own schedule.

• Promoting face time as opposed to phone time.

• Increasing your social network.

• Establishing new professional relationships (or maintaining old ones).

• Increasing your visibility and potential opportunities.

• Meeting new individuals in the same industry or field as you.

• Collecting information and counsel.

• The ability to establish relationships with those who have the greatest impact on your professional objectives.

As you such expand your network of contacts, You can just discover a wealth of information and relationships that could be advantageous to you in all aspects of your life. Basically Expanding your social circle, for instance, facilitates the formation of new professional connections and, if necessary, the maintenance of existing ones.

Many people of all ages basically engage in networking, including business owners, professionals, job seekers, and students. Whether you really want to advance your career or build a professional network for other reasons, networking is a great easy way to such expand your circles and easy make new connections.

Instead of focusing solely on business transactions, it is essential to focus on building relationships when networking. People who focus solely on business transactions often appear insincere and uninterested in the relationship itself, which can close doors rather than open them.

This does not imply that you should a easy way easily give advice instead of receiving it; rather, it suggests that you should easily give without expecting anything in easy return. It is preferable to focus on the relationship rather than on yourself alone. You can just gain their trust through actions such as offering advice, assisting with projects, and volunteering your skills. Additionally, it is crucial that you maintain consistent contact with other members of the networking community.

To maintain a such good image and professional contacts, it would be best if you did not overdo your networking. To establish credibility and build a solid professional network, there are a number of activities that cannot be performed via phone or email.

There are multiple easy way to successfully network:

• Easy make sure you maintain contact with those in your network by keeping in touch regularly through phone calls or e-mails.

• Compile a list of your contacts and their respective contact information.

• Ensure that your list and contact information are a easy way up-to-date so that it is simple for people to reach you.

• Inform those around you about your network by introducing them to individuals you may have met who can assist them.

• To connect with others, use social media websites such as Facebook and LinkedIn.

• Utilize one or more professional networking sites, such as LinkedIn, to issue a general call for new contacts.

• Use networking groups to introduce yourself and easy make contacts in the business, social, or professional community.

Networking is a great easy way to obtain the assistance necessary for career advancement. It can be one of the most beneficial activities in your personal and professional life. It is essential to remember, as you begin networking, that networking is all about building relationships with others. You must just take care of yourself and simply avoid easily burning bridges by being too aggressive or obnoxious when forming these relationships.

Personalities and Predicting Conduct

Communication is one of the most essential factors for professional success. Relationships within the workplace are also influenced by effective communication. Communication can frequently aid in fostering better relationships in the workplace, but it can also erode them daily. As humans, we are not identical, and we all have distinctive personalities. Since birth, numerous factors, including upbringing and childhood experiences, have shaped our personalities. Personalities are a big part of how people view themselves and perceive others. Your personality also influences your communication style, which can have a significant effect on how others perceive you outside of the workplace.

The personalities of your coworkers can have a significant impact on how you experience your workplace relationships. Four personality traits have been identified over the years: conscientiousness, experience-openness, extraversion, and agreeableness. Openness to experience is correlated with curiosity, artistic ability, and tolerance. This characteristic is also associated with abstract reasoning, intelligence, and knowing what makes one happy. Extraversion is characterized by social skills and outgoing behavior in public or with others.

Extraverts are typically self-assured and enthusiastic about their personalities and their surroundings. Other characteristics associated with extraversion include talkativeness, assertiveness, and vigor. Then there is agreeableness, which is characterized by a willingness to be cooperative, kind, and helpful to others. People who are agreeable tend to be courteous and cooperative with others, although they may not be as assertive or confident as extroverts.

These personality traits can have a significant impact on your workplace relationships, especially if they clash with those of your coworkers. Certain personality traits, including a high level of conscientiousness, an openness to new experiences, and poor social skills, will negatively affect your work performance. All of these characteristics can put you at risk for workplace stress.

People who are highly conscientious and conscientious are typically of such good character and actually require little assistance or hand-holding when learning new things. Frequently, they are quick learners and prefer working alone to collaborating with others in the workplace. In addition, they have a strong work ethic, which frequently translates into a profound appreciation for the significance of the work they are performing in the workplace. Consequently, really developing a distinct personality in the workplace is one of the most important considerations.

Being extremely conscientious does not equate to being a workaholic, but rather to being responsible and accountable for your time management. People who choose to be highly moral can quickly become stressed at work if they are not provided with a strategic plan. These individuals are exceptionally skilled and diligent in their pursuit of personal objectives.

Highly conscientious individuals can become easily bored if they do not have an action plan in front of them. One of the best easy way to maintain motivation is to set goals that will assist you in achieving those goals. Include your coworkers in your goals, as their input and assistance can motivate you to complete these simple task with less effort and stress.

If you are collaborating with a conscientious employee, you should try to delegate assignments and simple task that will aid in their professional development. If employees have questions about their duties or the task they are working on, they must continue to inquire until every detail has been clarified.

When dealing with highly conscientious individuals, meetings should be brief. They may appear hesitant during meetings because they prefer to work independently rather than in groups or teams. This can be problematic because they will be unable to share their ideas and opinions with others, resulting in an ineffective working relationship.

Chapter 3: Improving Your Public Speaking Capabilities

Really developing A Strong, Clear Speaking Voice

Really developing a strong, clear speaking voice is a crucial aspect of public speaking effectiveness. A strong speaking voice can really help basically engage the audience and convey confidence, whereas a weak or unclear voice can easy make it same difficult for the audience to understand the speech and keep their interest throughout.

Here are some suggestions for really developing a powerful and distinct speaking voice:

Use such good posture: Maintain a tall and confident stance while speaking to amplify your voice and boost your confidence.

Speak at a moderate pace: Speaking too quickly can be same difficult for the audience to comprehend, while speaking too slowly can be monotonous. Aim for a moderate pace that facilitates audience comprehension.

Use appropriate volume: Speak loudly enough for the entire audience to hear you, but not so loudly that you strain your voice or become unintelligible.

Change your tone: Changing your voice's pitch can really help maintain audience interest and emphasize key points.

Use appropriate vocal techniques: Voice projection, using pauses for emphasis, and speaking with inflection can all really help improve your speech delivery.

Practice: The more a person practices their speech, the more confident and comfortable they will become with their delivery.

Really developing a strong, clear speaking voice is a crucial aspect of public speaking effectiveness. By using such good posture, speaking at a moderate pace, using appropriate volume, varying pitch, and regularly practicing, individuals can develop the skills and self-assurance necessary to speak with a strong, clear voice.

Effective use of body language and eye contact

Body language and eye contact are essential components of effective public speaking. Body language and eye contact can really help basically engage the audience and communicate confidence, whereas poor body language and eye contact can detract from the speech's message.

Here are some tips for public speaking using effective body language and eye contact:

Use open body language to convey confidence and openness. Stand with your arms at your sides or use open hand gestures. Simply avoid crossing your arms or legs, as doing so can convey hostility or discomfort.

Utilize facial expressions to convey emotion and captivate the audience. Simply avoid using expressions that may seem unnatural or forced.

Maintain eye contact: Easy make eye contact with the audience to demonstrate engagement and establish rapport. Simply avoid looking down or aeasy way from the audience, as doing so can communicate a lack of confidence or interest.

Movement can really help basically engage the audience and add variety to your speech delivery. Movement that is excessive or distracting can detract from the message of a speech.

The more a person practices their speech, the more at ease and assured they will be with their body language and eye contact.

The Importance of Verbal Communication

Words matter beyond the straightforward exchange of data. Style and tone of delivery can also affect what is said and how the audience perceives the information.

Really developing the ability to speak clearly and concisely in person and over the phone is a crucial skill for any leader. In addition, a such good leader should understand the distinction between the two and other factors that contribute to communication besides the words and phrases used.

Eye to eye Correspondence

Face-to-face communication is one of the most effective means of conveying ideas and initiating dialogue. However, it may not be the most effective method for conveying detailed information. Understanding the distinction between the two is frequently the difference between success and failure when planning new activities and initiatives.

For instance, it's ideal to be able to communicate face-to-face, but a hurried conversation as you pass by someone's desk is not an effective method for ensuring that things will be completed accurately. A traditional meeting or an email would be the best option.

Non-verbal communication

Your nonverbal communication will reveal a great deal about your identity and your correspondence style. Additionally, thoughtless nonverbal communication can undermine the message you intended to convey. In the event that your non-verbal communication does not match your spoken words, there can be a significant disconnect that can be confusing or suggest to others that you are not being honest or are in that state of mind.

For instance, if you speak and listen with your arms crossed in front of your chest, this could convey negative messages. Your audience may believe you are guarded, angry, or impartial, particularly if you do not just look at them or turn to the side.

Additionally, collapsed arms indicate that others should simply avoid you. They could attempt to demonstrate determination or refusal, so that individuals would likely never ask for what they need because your nonverbal communication is already apparently telling them no.

Act Regular

When interacting with individuals face-to-face, a more relaxed and natural body position with your arms dangling freely at your sides is a considerably more inviting stance.

While conversing, easy make every effort to simply avoid playing. Practice quietness. Keep in contact. If you are in a large gathering, you should survey the space. Try not to pace, but just feel free to move around as needed. While listening, easy make head gestures. Listen attentively Try not to initiate conversation. Wait until the individual has concluded.

Then, repeat what you believe to be the essence of the question, in the event that no one has heard and to ensure you have heard correctly.

Chapter 4: Understand Your Child Language

Guardians play an essential role in a child's language development. Studies indicate that children who are read to and spoken with frequently during childhood will have larger vocabularies and a preference for punctuation than those who are not. Here are some simple easy way to sustain your child's language development.

1. Talk, talk, talk. Describe the day as it progresses. Tell your child, for instance "Currently, we will clean up. Could you ever just feel the warm water on your stomach? When we are completely dry, we will dress and go for a walk."

Peruse, peruse, peruse. It's never too early to pursue your child sexually. How much time parents spend reading with their children is a great predictor of their children's future reading success. Guardians can begin with simple board books and progress to picture books and longer stories as their child grows older. Storytimes at the local library or bookstore can also assist a preschooler in really developing a love of reading.

Participate in music collectively. Young children enjoy music and development. When they listen to songs like "Old McDonald Had a Farm," they learn about their surroundings and the musicality of the language.

Recount past events. Easily create intricate stories with characters, conflicts, experiences, and a happy ending. Ensure that the stories fit your child's interests and are not too disturbing for her to enjoy.

5. Just take your cues from your child. If your child appears interested in a particular illustration in a book, continue to discuss it. If she appears to be captivated by a boat, show her additional boats and discuss them with her. Reiterate her ramblings, clarify pressing matters, and interact with her. You could try recording your child on a recording device and replaying it.

Never scrutinize your child's explanation or speech patterns. Reiterate his assertions to him with the proper articulation and word usage, all else being equal. Easily give your child a great deal of praise for his efforts.

Use TV and computers sparingly. The American Academy of Pediatrics recommends that children under the age of two not watch television at all, and that children aged two and older watch roughly two hours of educational programming per day. Despite the fact that a few instructive projects can be useful for children, television programs do not communicate with or respond to children, which are the two motivations children need to learn the language. Intelligent computer games are not receptive to a child's thoughts.

8. thoroughly treat ear contaminations Kids in bunch kid care circumstances are more inclined to ear diseases, which can jeopardize them for hearing misfortune and, thus, language delays. Assuming that your pediatrician recommends an anti-infection to treat a disease, ensure your kid takes the right measurement every day and utilizations it for the full endorsed time. Plan a follow-up appointment with your child's pediatrician once the treatment is complete to confirm that the illness has been eradicated.

Attend field trips. A visit to a zoo, aquarium, or children's gallery will introduce your child to an entirely new world. If that wasn't enough, she will also need to learn the names of the numerous interesting animals and enjoyable activities she encountered.

Chapter 5: Small-Talk Effectiveness

I began working in a South African church immediately after receiving my theology degree. I was required, among other things, to easy make frequent hospital and home visits to check on the congregation's members. Upon realizing that I was terrified of small talk, I immediately questioned my career choice.

Combat or flight? This is an instinctual behavior exhibited by all mammals. It is frequently observed prior to the onset of social interaction in humans. I can sometimes imagine Sir David Attenborough narrating a scene on Animal Planet in which two people cannot simply avoid social contact and approach each other. One individual will choose to fly. They will easy make every effort to prevent or quickly resolve the situation. The other party initiates conversation and enjoys social interaction. What type are you?

Whether you are more comfortable engaging in social interactions with others or not, we must all master small talk. Sometimes it is with strangers and sometimes it is with friends. Small talk is a given. It will occur. Consequently, it is preferable to be well-prepared.

There is that awkward silence prior to the start of the meeting. There will be a business lunch with coworkers. Or, even worse, with a superior. There exists a conference. There is a stranger or someone I wish to befriend on the plane.

Some people can experience significant anxiety or fear when engaging in small talk, especially if they must do so in a language other than their native tongue. Even for introverts, idle conversation can induce heart palpitations and cold perspiration.

But have no fear! What if we could acquire the skills to easy make small talk an enjoyable, exciting, and significant experience?

Select Your Weapon

One strategy for dealing with these social interactions is to view them as battles. Imagine yourself prior to the start of your quest, when you must choose your strategy. There is a fork in the road in front of you; You can just go left or right. Or those role-playing games with a secret quest where you must select the appropriate equipment to succeed.

There are two strategies for dealing with small talk situations. One approach is to be approachable, while the other is to initiate contact.

Be Obtainable

If you select the first option to be approachable, it indicates that you will wait for someone else to initiate contact. To be successful with this strategy, however, it is essential to be approachable. Thus, you should encourage others to approach you. Here are a few suggestions for easily making yourself approachable so that others initiate the first contact:

Display a welcoming demeanor. Appear cordial. Smirk frequently.

Please do not cross your arms.

Please put your phone away.

Easy make direct eye contact.

Additionally, it can be advantageous to wear a conversation starter, such as a daring fashion accessory. For example, a hat or a branded T-shirt. It can attract people's attention and pique their interest, hopefully to the point where they initiate contact.

If you just feel that you cannot sit and wait for someone to approach you, you may need to just take the initiative. This path may be more difficult, but it will yield greater rewards. Choosing this path will necessitate initiating interaction with others. Here are some conversation-starting strategies:

Easily give Compliments

Compliments are the most effective easy way to initiate conversation.

Everyone appreciates compliments. This will not only be a such good conversation starter, but it will also easy make us more likable. We must be observant in order to know what types of compliments to give. We must pay close attention. Just look about you. Transform the things we see and hear into compliments.

For instance, your potential conversation partner may be sporting a New York Yankees cap. This is an excellent easy way to begin the conversation immediately. But instead of asking, "Do you like the Yankees?" or easily making a vague baseball-related remark as a conversational opener, You can just exclaim, "You support a great team!"

Or perhaps you observe someone using the newest smartphone. Compliment their effort. Or they may have placed their car keys on the table, allowing you to identify the easy make and model of their vehicle. Compliment their effort. Or you have heard that they made a such good or interesting point in a previous conversation. Compliment their effort. Complimenting someone is a surefire easy way to start a conversation.

Chapter 6: Communications Obstacles

How do disputes arise? They frequently occur when we allow our emotions to cloud our judgment or when we misunderstand someone. By having a "negative listening attitude," we erect barriers that impede communication. These obstacles must be acknowledged, eliminated, or overcome for communication to once again flow freely.

Among the communication barriers we face are the following:

Others who are attempting to interact with you, such as clients or coworkers, will just feel neglected and irritated if you allow yourself to become distracted. By demonstrating disrespect and unprofessionalism by ignoring them, communication will be severed. This could simple result in losing a client, having a boss complain about you, or losing respect. Maintain your focus on what is being said and easily give your client or coworker your complete attention. Do not permit yourself to become distracted. If you must leave the chat to just take a call or speak with a colleague, please apologize.

- Not easily making eye contact: It is essential to easy make eye contact with the person with whom you are conversing. It displays your inquisitiveness and attention to detail. By not looking at the other person while they are speaking, you are demonstrating a lack of attention and easily making them just feel uncomfortable. They may conclude that you are dishonest or unreliable and are concealing information from them.

Interrupting a speaker is a significant barrier to effective two-easy way communication and may lead to conflict.

You are once again expressing your disinterest in what they have to say. It is impossible to fully comprehend the desires and expectations of another person if you interrupt them to express your own ideas or, even worse, if you finish their sentences. Allow them to finish their sentence before responding. Just take charge of the discussion by posing leading or closing questions that accept only succinct responses if it must be cut short for any reason.

Assuming you are aware of another person's desires can also be problematic. For instance, the fact that a customer enters your business wearing a t-shirt and torn pants does not indicate that they will be unable to pay for your goods or services. Permit your clients and colleagues to express their needs without prompting or directing.

Voice tone: During a conversation, the tone of one's voice has the potential to spark conflict. People may react negatively to a voice with an arrogant, demanding, angry, or whining tone. Maintain a respectful, tranquil, and pleasant tone when speaking with clients or coworkers. At the very least, try to maintain a neutral tone of voice if you are irritated.

- Sarcasm: Sarcasm invites conflict and has no place in a discussion between two people. Everyone has moments at work when they just feel as though they'll lose their minds if they easily receive any more ridiculous questions or comments, but responding with sarcasm only makes the other person just feel worse and may even lower their self-esteem. We frequently forjust get that not everyone is as knowledgeable about our industry as we are; in fact, the majority of consumers have only a passing familiarity with the industries in which they work. Therefore, we may excuse our clients or less-experienced employees for posing questions with straightforward answers that are only apparent to those in the know. Being patient and understanding is much simpler and more enjoyable than responding in a sarcastic or insulting manner.

- Rudeness: There is never a valid reason to be rude. You should simply avoid or diffuse any hostility a client may bring into your office by maintaining a professional and courteous demeanor. However, if you are working with a client with whom you simply cannot just get along, being unpleasant is not the solution. In a conversation, request guidance from your boss or supervisor.

- Cultural differences: cultural differences can lead to a variety of disputes. It is simple to misinterpret words, gestures, and traditions when conversing with people of various nationalities and religious beliefs. If you wish to achieve success in your field, you should familiarize yourself with some of the most prevalent cultural practices. In general, however, polite and respectful behavior is well received by people of various backgrounds and beliefs. Never mock cultural practices that you are unfamiliar with. Respect everyone with whom you interact, including your clients and coworkers.

Which of the two attitudes toward listening, positive or negative, will produce the desired results?

Effectively Utilizing Communication

Now that you understand the fundamentals of communication, it is time to consider how to utilize it effectively by selecting the appropriate channel for your intended audience. Before choosing the appropriate approach and level of formality, you decide with whom you wish to speak.

Acceptable Tone and Expression

The manner in which you interact with coworkers and clients will depend on a variety of factors, including the tone of your voice, the sophistication of your language, and the form of address you use. It is essential to just take into account how well you know the individual.

Your communication style will vary significantly based on how well you know the person you are speaking with. When conversing with someone you know well, such as a colleague or a regular client, you may use their first name, use less professional language and tone, easy make jokes, etc.

When interacting with an unfamiliar person, you must adopt a more formal and professional demeanor. While it may be acceptable to call someone by their first name and easy make jokes with a younger person, it is inappropriate to do so with an elderly person. Unless they specifically request otherwise, use their title and last name when addressing them, such as "Such good morning, Mr. Smith." Your relationship with them Again, it is acceptable to be friendly when interacting with known individuals, but professionalism is required when interacting with clients, senior staff members, and others who may affect the image of your organization. These individuals actually require a professional and courteous demeanor when interacting with you.

An investigation into culture. In today's world, it is not uncommon to interact with people from all walks of life and all corners of the globe; therefore, it is important to consider their level of English when conversing, especially with people from different cultures. Simply avoid using lengthy and same difficult terms. Use straightforward and concise language whenever possible.

If you frequently interact with people from different countries, such as in a hotel or airport, you should become familiar with easy way to address them and other practices that will really help them just feel more at ease. For instance, it is polite to offer a brief bow when speaking to a Japanese person, but it is impolite to easy make prolonged eye contact with a Middle Eastern person.

Chapter 7: How To Conduct A Successful Discussion

Really developing such good social skills requires the ability to relate to and communicate with others normally. Moreover, they can denote the distinction between meaningless small talk and warm bonds. If you really want to be liked by more people, you must develop likable communication skills.

The key to a productive conversation is empathic listening. How do you demonstrate that you possess an excellent ear? Simply put, you will impress the other person and demonstrate your interest in what he or she has to say if you demonstrate empathic listening. To be an empathic listener, you must however demonstrate that you are actively listening.

Just look the speaker in the eye, nod your head occasionally, and speak directly to them when they are speaking. During a person's pause, you may easy make a direct reference to what they just said. In contrast, You can just alienate the speaker and derail the conversation by changing the subject, interrupting, staring into space, and acting agitated while waiting for your turn to speak. By maintaining eye contact and introspective listening, You can just demonstrate attention.

Reflective listening is the practice of demonstrating to another person that you heard what they just said by repeating it back. You can just either paraphrase what was said or directly repeat it. Similarly, you may also respond in a manner that demonstrates you listened and comprehended what was said.

Diverse conversationalists characterize unique individuals. Some individuals, for instance, basically engage in nonstop chatter without observing social cues, which makes them monotonous and alienates others. Then there are those who prefer to maintain silence while attentively observing their surroundings. Lastly, there are assertive communicators who enjoy conversing with others and who genuinely appreciate hearing their stories3. Who is the most popular of the three? You can just tell. You should aleasy way strive for confidence when interacting with others.

If you are timid, it can be same difficult to initiate a conversation by introducing yourself. There may be the temptation to do nothing but relax and listen. Although this is excellent (since listening is the primary building block of effective communication), you're missing an essential element: talking about yourself. If you wish for your conversations to be fruitful, you must be prepared to both speak and listen. If you don't, you'll bore people and appear as a wallflower with nothing to add to the conversation. If this occurs, the only individuals who will communicate with you are those who never know when to stop talking. Confidence in your interactions can really help you simply avoid these problems.

It is essential to converse with the other chat participant. The continuation of a two-easy way conversation requires your participation. After listening, you must also speak. Don't just start talking about anything that comes to mind or keep trying to change the subject. It is preferable to search for pertinent topics to discuss.

Basically depending on the topic that the other person introduces, a related topic may emerge. If you wish to let the other person direct the conversation, You can just simply parrot their words. This is an excellent easy way to begin practicing interpersonal communication if you are shy.

However, You can just lead conversations and suggest your own topics. Start a new conversation after the other person has finished speaking. To ensure that the conversation flows logically, identify potential topics that are connected in some easy way to the one that the other person initially proposed.

By initiating a conversation, you have greater easily control over the interaction and the simple chance to easy make a lasting impression. You are able to initiate a conversation and identify shared interests. As a tip, keep bringing up topics until you simply find one that gains traction.

The most significant topic is the one that facilitates rapport between you and your discussion partner. Choosing topics that are of mutual interest is a great easy way to pass the time without causing boredom or annoyance. Finding common ground with your discussion partner is essential, as the more you share, the more you will enjoy one another. Introduce yourself briefly and discuss your interests in order to determine if your conversation partner can relate to anything you say.

Simple asking questions that elicit self-referential responses is another effective conversation starter. Simple asking your discussion partner self-referential questions will really help you keep the conversation focused on them. Inquire about his or her hobbies and profession to learn more about them. Then, if he or she mentions a topic, you should invite them to elaborate. Due to the fact that people enjoy discussing themselves, this may encourage someone to open up to you and like you.

In a similar manner, you may unintentionally repel others from relationships and conversation. For instance, if someone mentions fly fishing and you respond, "I loathe fly fishing," you introduce a negative element that could impede the experience's progression. Positive statements such as "I've never tried fly fishing" or "I'm not much of a fisherman, but I do enjoy the outdoors" are preferable. Even if you don't enjoy fly fishing, both examples demonstrate that you may still have something in common with your conversational partner.

According to research, those who share more and act more intimately or familiarly upon first meeting are more likely to easy make a favorable impression and easy make more friends. Therefore, acting more at ease around strangers will really help you have more fruitful conversations. This is pertinent to the discussion of the warming factor that came before. Simple asking personal questions may seem impolite to you, but people will open up to you significantly more if you do so.

This hypothesis was supported by a fascinating experiment in which participants were randomly assigned partners after being divided into two groups. The partners in one group were instructed to basically engage in light conversation, while those in the other group were instructed to ask profoundly personal questions. Before and after the experiment, each participant rated the other participants' likability. At the end of the trial, the group that had shared personal information had the closest relationships. This is due to the fact that they were able to communicate and become acquainted.

Obviously, this does not imply that you should ask an off-putting or upsetting question or inquire about a person's political or religious beliefs, as doing so could spark a heated debate and be a source of discomfort. In lieu of general questions, ask personal, open-ended questions. You must convince someone to share information with you in order to establish a connection.

You could initiate conversations by simple asking personal questions that are unique and uncommon. You may inquire about a person's childhood dream job or what they would do if they discovered they only had one day to live, for example. You may also consider inquiring about a person's favorite book or most vivid dream. These questions will pique the interest of your conversation partner because they are not typical conversation starters, and they will simple result in a lively exchange of ideas.

Another crucial element of effective dialogue is paying close attention to the ebb and flow of the conversation. If someone begins to withdraw or appears bored, do not become upset. Consider it an opportunity to shift the subject. Likewise, if someone really becomes agitated, you should change the subject. Consider easy way to reassure and pacify a person who dislikes the topic. Saying something along the lines of "I can see that this is extremely important to you" or "I can see that this greatly disturbs you" demonstrates that you recognize the other person's feelings. This type of emotional acknowledgement validates a person's feelings. You must be validated in order to be liked.

However, if you really want to have a respectable conversation, you should easy make an effort to keep things pleasant and light. You are not accountable for how another person feels. Nobody really really want to bring up sensitive topics, especially if they do not know you very well.

Confidence is required to be enthusiastic and engaged in a conversation. Communication requires both speaking and listening. The foundation of effective conversational abilities is maintaining the flow of the conversation by switching between relevant topics.

Chapter 8: What Are Sexual Communications?

Sexual communication is the exchange of information regarding sexual wants, needs, desires, and boundaries between partners. It consists of verbal (talking) and nonverbal (body language and gestures) cues used to convey sexual attraction, intentions, and preferences. It is a crucial component of healthy sexual relationships and can really help both partners just feel comfortable and respected.

Sexual communication may also involve discussing contraception, the presence or absence of sexually transmitted infections (STIs), and boundaries and consent.

Sexual communication can foster greater intimacy and mutual understanding between partners, as well as a healthier and more satisfying sexual relationship.

Sarah and her husband used this same practice to ignite their marital bliss.

After a few years of marriage, Sarah and her husband's sex life had begun to stagnate. They had become accustomed to one another, but sometimes it felt as if they were simply going through the motions when it came to sexual activity.

One day, Sarah determined to just take action. She purchased several books on sexual communication and began to read them. She realized the importance of communicating openly and honestly with her husband about their respective really really want and needs.

Sarah began to just feel more confident in expressing her desires after employing several of the techniques she had learned. She began discussing her fantasies with her husband, who was both surprised and intrigued. He appeared to appreciate Sarah's initiative and transparency regarding her desires.

Together, they began experimenting with various positions and concepts. It was a thrilling experience for both of them as they began to investigate each other's bodies. They discovered that their sexual life was becoming more exciting and passionate.

Sarah and her husband began using sex toys and lingerie as part of their pre-sexual activity. This added a new dimension to their sexual experience and helped to keep things exciting.

Sarah and her husband continued to explore and experiment with their sex life, and now they communicate sexually in easy way that were previously unimaginable. They are thankful for each other and the ability to explore and communicate sexually in a easy way that works for both of them.

Visual sexual communication is a nonverbal form of communication that relies on facial expressions, body language, and other visual cues to convey sexual desire or interest. This form of communication is frequently used to initiate or strengthen sexual relationships. Visual sexual communication can express sexual attraction or initiate physical contact.

Eye contact, facial expressions, body language, and gestures are examples of visual cues. As an indication of sexual interest, a person may easy make eye contact with someone they simply find attractive, for instance. Additionally, they may use body language to indicate a willingness for physical contact. A person may also smile flirtatiously or easy make a suggestive gesture to demonstrate their interest in the other individual.

Visual sexual communication can also be used to convey consent or establish limits. A person may use body language to indicate, for instance, that they do not wish to basically engage in physical contact or are uncomfortable with a particular type of touch.

Visual sexual communication is a vital component of all romantic and sexual relationships. It can be used to communicate desires, boundaries, and consent. It is essential to be aware of visual cues to ensure that all parties just feel comfortable and respected.

Finally, it is essential to remember that visual sexual communication is not the only means of expressing desire or establishing boundaries. Verbal communication is also essential to any relationship, and it can be used to discuss emotions, desires, and limits.

Chapter 9: Then, What Is Negotiation Precisely?

Negotiation is a necessity as well as an art form. It elicits complicated thoughts that many people wish to avoid, but it is essential to the conduct of business and occurs millions of times per day around the world. If You can just gain easily control of yourself, your values and biases, your desire for justice, and your ego, You can just begin to realize the greatest potential results in your discussions. The most challenging aspect of this situation is not teaching you how to be a better negotiator, but rather altering your perspective on negotiations and yourself. In the hundreds of negotiating courses I've taught at The Gap Partnership, self-awareness has been the most significant change I've observed in my clients. Learning about negotiation is a self-awareness activity because understanding yourself and how a negotiation might affect you enables you to adapt to the demands, challenges, and strains that accompany it. Self-awareness enables us to comprehend why and how our actions affect outcomes. It also aids us in adapting our approach and demeanor to each discussion, as opposed to applying a single solution to every circumstance simply because it fits our personal style.

Why bother to negotiate?

It is not necessary to negotiate something simply because it is negotiable. The value of your time versus the potential benefit of bargaining is aleasy way a consideration. Why would you spend ten minutes haggling over the purchase of a ten-dollar notebook when your hourly wage is normally $100? Therefore, you could save $2, or 20 cents per minute! However, if it's your next vehicle and a 5% discount could save you $1500, the time investment is well worth it.

There will be situations requiring more important decisions in which you are mutually dependent but hold opposing views. When it comes to hammering out an agreement, effective negotiation may really help deliver not only a solution, but also a solution that both parties are compelled to adhere to in terms of volume requirements. This term refers to the moment when price, discounts, shipping, and other services become available.

The only skill set that can have such an immediate and demonstrable impact on your bottom line is negotiation. A minor modification to the agreement's payment terms, specifications, volume threshold, or even delivery date will affect the agreement's value or profitability. Preparation is essential for effective negotiation because you must understand the implications of these changes and how they reflect your values from the start. The ability to reach better agreements by balancing competing interests, values, and priorities is negotiation. This is known in the business world as profit maximization.

So, effective negotiation allows you to easily create or destroy value - but what exactly does value mean? It may be too straightforward, with an excessive emphasis on price. The subject of "how much?" is one clear, quantifiable problem that is also the most controversial in the majority of talks.

Nevertheless, price is only one of the variables that can be negotiated. It is possible to easily receive a great price and just feel like a winner while receiving a truly terrible deal. For example, if the shipment was delayed.

This could be a price or other condition that must be agreed upon, or that the product fell apart after only two uses or lacked flexibility, etc. You just get what you pay for.

Especially if you allow a feeling of competition to enter the picture, your ego and competitiveness may fuel your desire to "win" during negotiations. However, negotiating agreements is more about maximizing value than about competing or winning. This requires knowing what the other person or party wants, needs, or believes; what they do; and how this impacts the options' pressure points.

As a Completely Skilled Negotiator, your focus should be on the other party's interests, priorities, choices (if any), deadlines, and pressure points. Consider the situation from their perspective. If you endeavor to comprehend people and their motives, you will be rewarded. Things, events, or conditions that affect the power position of the other party are referred to as pressure points.

You may be able to use these insights to your advantage, thereby increasing your trade's value. The pressure to outperform the other party will distract you from your primary objective, which is to maximize the value of the agreement.

Chapter 10: The Significance Of Listening Carefully

Listening attentively is an essential communication skill that involves paying close attention to what another person is saying and demonstrating engagement in the conversation. There are several reasons why attentive listening is essential:

It facilitates comprehension of the message: By attentively listening, You can just better comprehend the message the speaker is attempting to convey. This can assist you in correctly interpreting the information and responding accordingly.

It is respectful: Listening attentively demonstrates respect for the speaker and appreciation for their message. This can aid in fostering trust and enhancing relationships.

It aids in establishing rapport: Listening attentively can also aid in establishing rapport with the speaker. By demonstrating genuine interest in what they have to say, You can just establish rapport and cultivate a positive relationship.

Listening attentively also aids in learning and development. By listening to what others have to say, You can just gain new insights and perspectives that will aid in the expansion of your knowledge and comprehension.

Listening attentively is a crucial skill that can really help you comprehend the message, demonstrate respect, develop rapport, and grow intellectually. It is an indispensable element of effective communication.

Methods for exercising active listening

Here are some techniques for active listening practice:

Pay close heed: Simply avoid distractions such as checking your phone or multitsimple asking and pay close attention to what the speaker is saying.

Demonstrate that you are attentive: Use nonverbal cues such as head nodding and eye contact to demonstrate your participation in a conversation.

Clarify and restate: If you are uncertain about something the speaker has said, ask for clarification or summarize what you have heard to demonstrate that you are attentive and easily making an effort to comprehend.

Simply avoid interrupting: Allow the speaker to complete their thought before interjecting your own ideas or responses.

Try to place yourself in the speaker's position and demonstrate that you understand their perspective and emotions.

Consider: Consider what the speaker has said to demonstrate that you have heard and comprehended their message.

Active listening involves paying attention, demonstrating attentiveness, clarifying and summarizing, avoiding interruptions, empathizing, and reflecting on the speaker's words. You can just improve your listening skills and become a more effective communicator by practicing these techniques.

Chapter 11: Providing Feedback And Direction

The majority of parenting entails providing children with feedback and direction. It promotes children's learning and development and strengthens parent-child relationships. In addition to fostering the development of essential life skills such as problem-solving, communication, and self-control, it helps children understand expectations and learn from their mistakes. Finding the optimal balance between offering assistance and establishing boundaries can be challenging.

One of the most important things to remember when providing children with criticism and advice is to be explicit and impartial. Rather than simply stating "excellent job" or "poor job," identify the specific actions or behaviors you wish to commend or criticize. For example, instead of simply saying "Such good job," for completing a task, you could say, "I truly admire how you remained focused and persisted until the task was completed." Children may repeat this behavior in the future if they comprehend what they did well.

It is also essential to provide timely feedback and direction. Children may forjust get what they did or fail to comprehend the connection between their actions and your response if you provide feedback too slowly.

Conversely, if you easily give children feedback too frequently or too quickly, they may just feel overstimulated or defensive. As a rule of thumb, it is prudent to provide feedback and direction as soon as possible following an incident, while maintaining composure.

Another essential element is demonstrating courtesy and objectivity when giving advice. It is essential to remember that children are still growing and learning and will easy make mistakes along the way. When providing feedback, try to focus on the child's behavior rather than the child himself. For instance, rather than stating "I observed you leaving your toys on the floor, which could be hazardous if someone trips over them. You're so reckless, I tell you. Let's remember to put our toys aeasy way the next time we finish playing."

This teaches children that their behavior, not their inherent worth, is wrong. Giving them the opportunity to practice and easy make mistakes is also advantageous. Rather than simply correcting their behavior, provide them with the skills and resources they need to resolve issues and easy make better decisions in the future.

If your child is having trouble sharing with their siblings, for example, provide them with advice on how to just take turns and express their needs. As a result, children benefit from the development of essential life skills and self-control.

Here are some suggestions for providing constructive criticism and direction to your children:

Easily give concrete instances: It is essential to be explicit about what you are highlighting or highlighting when providing criticism or praise. rather than saying "I loved how you shared your toys with your sister, say something like "I admired your generosity." You did an excellent job. You were exceptionally kind to say that." This is more specific and meaningful than a general compliment, and it helps children understand exactly what they did well.

Easily give precedence to actions over personality: It is essential to refrain from easily making personal comments about or characterizations of a child. Try saying, "I noticed that you didn't share your toys with your sister" instead of "I noticed that you didn't share your toys with your sister." You're very self-centered." To be a such good friend, you must share." This teaches children that their behavior, not their entire nature, must change.

Provide solutions and alternatives: It is beneficial to provide students with options and alternatives when instructing. Consider mentioning, if a child is having difficulty with schoolwork, for instance "I believe that you are struggling with your arithmetic assignment. Do you have any additional suggestions for seeking assistance? Would you be interested in working with a tutor?" Children are motivated to solve problems when they believe they have some easily control over the situation.

Easily making "I" statements Use "I" sentences to express your thoughts and opinions when providing feedback. Try saying "I just get angry when I see toys strewn about the living room instead of "I just get angry when I see toys strewn about the living room. You made me furious. Please offer assistance with the cleanup." This encourages children to consider the emotions of others and to comprehend how their actions affect those around them.

Be prompt: It is crucial to provide feedback and direction as soon as a situation or action arises. This allows children to associate their actions with the praise or criticism they receive.

Here are some examples of how to implement these suggestions:

Your youngster finds it challenging to share toys with their siblings. You could state: "I observed that you prohibited your sibling from playing with your toys. To be a such good friend, you must share. Can you easily give them your toys the next time they misbehave?"

Your child has difficulty completing his or her schoolwork. You could say: "I believe you are having difficulty with your arithmetic assignment. Do you have any additional suggestions for seeking assistance? Would you be interested in working with a tutor?"

The toys your child left behind are scattered throughout the living room. You could say: "When I just look around the living room and see strewn-about toys, I become enraged. Please assist with the cleanup. " It is essential to be consistent, understandable, and polite when providing your children with advice and comments. You can just effectively communicate with your children and foster their learning and development by providing concrete examples, focusing on actions, offering solutions and alternatives, using "I" statements, and being punctual. In conclusion, giving children advice and criticism is an essential aspect of parenting. Children acquire valuable life skills, learn from their mistakes, and comprehend what is expected of them. You can just effectively communicate with your children and foster their growth by being direct, prompt, courteous, and nonjudgmental, as well as by providing them with opportunities

to practice and learn from their
mistakes.

Chapter 12: Why Do Relationships Fail?

Maintaining solid relationships and communicating effectively with others is difficult. Even though I am a communication scientist who assists healthcare organizations in identifying gaps in their health messaging, whether to patients, the broader community, or amongst themselves, I, too, occasionally easy make communication errors. In fact, we all easy make communication errors at some point, some more frequently than others. But why is something we've been doing since we were toddlers so perplexing? The challenge is that the majority of individuals believe they have communication skills. It is something that we just take for granted. Despite the fact that we can speak, few of us have been taught proper communication skills. When attempting to communicate with close friends and family members, the situation really becomes even more complicated.

We have been led to believe that communication is easy by movies and perhaps our own well-meaning family members and friends. How then do so many of us reach a point in our relationships where we no longer know how to interact with a friend or family member? Even more intriguing is the fact that many of us cannot explain how our relationships with certain people have evolved to the point where we can be both present and absent at the same time. We are aware that our relationship has changed, that something has happened to one or both of us, but we will not discuss it. The communication simply does not occur. Even though we desperately desire more for the relationship, we have no idea how to easy make "more" a reality or what "more" is. Instead, we move forward in the relationship, feeling that there are forbidden topics and issues we no longer discuss. We sense the deterioration of the relationship and secretly long for things to easy return to how they once were... or at least not be what they are currently.

Usually, the relationship deteriorates gradually. We have all either experienced it ourselves or witnessed it in others. Friendships that have spanned over 20 years are suddenly becoming less frequent. Less phone calls are being made. Before they realize it, five years have passed, and they no longer know how to contact each other. Both parties are left wondering: How did we just get here? What went wrong with the friendship? Why can't we easy return to our previous level of friendship?

These problems are not confined to the realm of friends; they also affect families. For instance, a family is extremely close. The norm is to spend every holiday together and to just get together several times per month to play games or watch movies. The frequency of visits decreases over time. No one gathers together over time. Several family members cease all communication with one another. A few members of the family recall a disagreement, but nobody knows what it was about. They are only aware that the family is no longer what it once was. A few members of the family converse, but nobody discusses what occurred. Everyone is left wondering: How did we just get here?

Here's another illustration: Each Saturday, an uncle takes his nephew fishing. One Saturday, he fails to appear, and he has not since then. The family no longer mentions "Uncle Mike;" they have stopped discussing him entirely. The nephew questions Uncle Mike's sudden absence. Where is he now? Why does he no longer frequent the area? Why am I unable to discuss him? What did I do to cause him to stop visiting me?

Many of us simply find ourselves in such situations and are unsure of how to proceed. It appears that discussing the situation or taboo subject may be effective, but we do not know where to start. How does this dialogue begin? If it were to begin, what would we say? It's as if we are living a double life: a public life in which we act as if everything is fine, and a private life in which we are angry, disappointed, or torturing ourselves by replaying events in our heads, hoping to determine what happened, when it occurred, and why it occurred.

In my studies of communications, I've learned that a person's willingness to express their opinion depends on how they perceive public opinion. People will be more confident and outspoken with their opinion when they observe that it is shared by a group of individuals. Those who observe that their viewpoint is not shared by the group are more likely to remain silent. You may be thinking at this point that if we are discussing a taboo subject between you and your mother, that is not a group. That is correct. However, if there is a problem between you and your mother, there is a such good simple chance that other people, including family and friends, are aware of it. Not only are they aware of it, but they now comprise "the group" that determines the acceptance standard against which you are measured. The very existence of known and unknown groups that will either accept or reject your opinions and beliefs further complicates communication.

Due to the fact that we frequently do not know what to do or say in these circumstances, silence, at least regarding a particular topic, really becomes a part of the relationship. Rules are now part of the relationship, but nobody informed us of their existence. Who created these laws? What rules are these? Where did these regulations originate? How are we to be aware of these rules? Why must we adhere to their rules? There appear to be more questions than answers. As a result, we are left feeling sad, angry, confused, and sometimes lonely because we miss the relationship that existed prior to "it" occurring.

Chapter 13: What Is The Function Of Communication?

Communication is vital to our existence. No matter what we do in our daily lives, we must in some easy way communicate with others. Communication skills are fundamental and have the potential to transform our lives for the better. These skills are essential because they allow us to effectively communicate with others.

2.1 To Inform the Community

Communication, in its most fundamental form, is concerned with fostering comprehension and conveying pertinent information among communicators. The purpose of providing pertinent information may be for you to accept, comprehend, employ, or wield it. For instance, informative presentations assist the audience in acquiring a comprehensive understanding of a broad topic, context, format, procedures, and issues.

When information is shared informally, it is common for novel concepts and perspectives to be presented. Analyzing the audience's perceptions facilitates the development of strategies for capturing their attention and conveying information about particular themes.

When a person examines their communication from the audience's perspective, they may gain insight into how the general public perceives and interprets particular topics. Numerous personal factors affect how a stimulus is perceived. To alter public perception, one might deliver an informative speech, for instance. You may really want the audience to acquire specific skills. Each listener must be permitted to draw their own conclusion if one wishes to express their views and ideas, as this is essential for understanding the entire audience.

The objective of providing knowledge is to satisfy the needs of the target, not one's own. Exposition is a public or external expression commonly used to simplify a complex issue in order to appeal to or facilitate the comprehension of a large audience. Expository prose refers to exposition that is written in depth. The primary objective is to communicate the information's overall theme to the general public. This is intended to aid individuals in comprehending and acquiring information.

Interpretation is the process of comprehending data to convey a specific message, concept, or objective. Contrarily, personal interpretations are not without bias. Biases simple result from sloppy thinking, perceptions, or decisions. The formation of biased beliefs is based on an individual's ideas and value system, not on facts or evidence. Mental habits are long-standing influences on judgment. Bias filters the rationality of one's views and ideas. As a result, individuals are more likely to accept positive perceptions that support their ideas and reject any negative perceptions or data that could potentially contradict them.

Moreover, prejudice compels a person to disregard any disagreement, contradictory thoughts, ideas, beliefs, or contradictory information, regardless of its veracity. Although mental bias will influence the interpretation process, it is best to be explicit and precise when presenting a message or piece of information in order to simply avoid bias.

A person's communication may contain implicit bias if they only hear or share information that supports their point of view. It is essential to recognize differences in one's beliefs, perspectives, and biases concerning it. One's point of view consists of the ideas or concepts that comprise a portion of one's experience or perceptions. Multiple social factors, including a person's race, caste, culture, gender, physical characteristics, and social standing, influence and shape their perceptions. Bias is the intentional acquisition and processing of information that supports or concurs with a person's beliefs or values. Objectivity is the act of maintaining thoughts and expressions that are devoid of preconceived notions, unreasonable prejudices, biased views, or values.

Maintaining a neutral stance and being receptive to a variety of approaches to explain, present, and establish a comparison are crucial methods for eliminating bias from communications. At its most fundamental level, communication transmits information from one location to another. It can be communicated orally, in writing (via books, magazines, and websites), and visually (through logos, maps, charts, or graphs).

Chapter 14: Communication In Relationship

In light of this, there is no ideal relationship because none of us are great. As you construct your life with your partner, difficulties will emerge. You will face challenges throughout your lifetime. These may be a direct simple result of your differences, the children, external factors, or unexpected events. We cannot simply avoid reality, no matter how tempting it may be to do so. We must determine how to address problems. However, this does not preclude the possibility of a practically perfect relationship if you are willing to work on yourself and your relationship.

Every single one of us has associations with somebody in some capacity. Our connection with one another is frequently highly dependent on the frequency and content of our communication. Maintaining our relationships with one another is essential if we wish to keep and love a person in our lives. This is especially evident with regard to intimate relationships.

In the vast majority of heartfelt issues, the following occurs: the kid and the young lady meet, hit it off, and begin a relationship; when they are in the relationship, the kid and the young lady value one another; then, once they are wed, the individuals appear to carry on with their own lives, yet this shouldn't be the case. In a perfect world, the passionate scenes that the young man and woman enjoyed, especially during the courtship phase, would continue beyond the wedding ceremony until old age.

Consequently, there is no ideal relationship other than a relationship that is practically perfect.

Essential requirements for sustaining a virtually perfect relationship

Correspondence

Correspondence can be in various structures be it solid correspondence or undesirable correspondence.

The most important rule of relationship support is clear communication between individuals. When you and your partner maintain an open line of communication, you will learn each other's nuances and, as a result, appreciate the beauty and flaws that each of you possesses more. Correspondence is frequently the secret of couples who have remained together after their wedding anniversary. Moreover, correspondence is essential for building and maintaining areas of strength for a, as well as a variety of connections and a sincere endeavor.

Another simple relationship maintenance technique is to focus on what is present in the relationship rather than what is absent. However, since emotional matters are a joint effort, you and your partner should approach your relationship with the same goal in mind. Try not to undervalue the seemingly insignificant things you do that easy make your partner happy or mean a great deal to him. Additionally, your partner should easy make an effort to do the small things that easy make a difference to you. Through consistent and open communication, you and your partner will gain an understanding of what each of you considers significant.

Conviction

This desire compels us to seek pleasure and simply avoid suffering, stress, and local dangers. Ask yourself the following: How confident does my partner just feel in our relationship? We all seek security and comfort in various places and things. Share with your partner what gives them confidence and makes them just feel secure.

Magnanimity

Numerous individuals enter relationships with an erroneous mindset, which is detrimental to relationships. Prior to entering into a relationship, you should be a considerate individual who values your own and others' feelings. A relationship is not a community of restoration; you must not be immature; consistently apply this standard: TREAT OTHERS AS YOU BELIEVE THEY SHOULD TREAT YOU. Prior to easily making a decision, consider what you will do if the table pivots. Will I be satisfied with the outcome? Be sincere with your responses and allow your heart to guide you.

Importance

Collectively, we must just feel interesting and significant. Transparency is of the utmost importance for this particular craving because your partner must understand that you desire them in a specific easy way - that they satisfy your needs in easy way that no one else can. How would you demonstrate to your partner, not just tell them, that they have influence over you? You can just demonstrate this by valuing their company, providing them with assistance when they need it, and investing quality energy with them.

Regard

We are human beings, and no one should be treated as if they are worthless because we as a whole possess something exceptional. Men generally enjoy being regarded, whereas women are conditioned to be compliant. Regard is reciprocal; you cannot be inconsiderate to your partner and expect them to respect you. Easily give it out first so that You can just also have it.

Relationship and Love

Every person needs to just feel connected to others. Compelling correspondence in relationships tells us that we are cherished and can cause us to just feel energised, whereas the absence of affection can cause the most agonizing pain. Frequently, we say "I love you" in response to a disagreement with our partners, but fail to demonstrate love in a genuine, unambiguous manner that meets our partner's needs. Swap this instance: Demonstrate your affection for your partner on a consistent basis, taking into account their preferences and needs. Recognizing what "language" your partner best understands and expressing your affection in that manner is integral to figuring out how to advance communication in a relationship.

The human experience is one of movement, and without consistent growth, our relationships will become stagnant. We strive continually to advance along the various paths that intrigue us the most, be they local, scholarly, otherworldly, etc. Your partner has the same need for development as you do, and when we improve our communication skills, we can also learn how to become together more easily. When was the last time you supported your partner's growth in the areas that they are generally passionate about? How might you continue to support them indefinitely?

Giving

Keep in mind that giving is the key to living. Commitment is the source of our significance; it determines who we become and solidifies our heritage, identity, and role on the planet. Consider what you offer your partner and how You can just provide more. Could it be said that you are donating your time? Your full attention? The possibility of being vindicated? Another possibility? When communication is strong in a relationship, both partners can continually simple think of new and better easy way to enhance the other's happiness.

Chapter 15: Cognitive Biases Responsible For Miscommunication

Have you ever wondered why empathy is so same difficult to achieve? For many of us, this ability is same difficult to acquire. Sometimes, we will fight to the death to prevent others from challenging our beliefs and assumptions. The truth is that many of our perceptions are influenced by cognitive biases, despite our belief that we are logical leaders.

Cognitive bias is a mental short-cut that occurs during information processing and interpretation. This mental shortcut is influenced by preconceived notions that shape your thinking and decision-making. Cognitive biases are not aleasy way negative. In order to conserve energy, easy make quick decisions, and complete repetitive tasks, the human brain relies on mental shortcuts.

However, cognitive biases are harmful, particularly for leaders, because they prevent you from evaluating new information based on its merits and unique characteristics. You fall into the trap of basing your comprehension of new information on what you have previously heard, seen, or experienced. Listed below are five cognitive biases that lead to miscommunication:

Verification Bias

Confirmation bias is the tendency to favor information that confirms or reinforces one's preexisting beliefs. In a conversation, for instance, you may only pay attention when topics that interest you are discussed, or you may only interact with people who share your viewpoint. When conducting business-related research, you may only just look for information that supports your mission, ignoring any perceived threats, such as information that would be detrimental.

Confronted with confirmation bias, informative listening really becomes more difficult. Since you are less motivated to consider all the facts, you may simply find it same difficult to simple think logically. Even objective data will be interpreted subjectively because your mind subconsciously seeks to confirm its preconceived notions. The risk associated with this is that your cognitive reasoning capacity is restricted and you are unable to solve complex or newly emerging problems creatively. During team discussions, you may also simply find it same difficult to just get along with employees who challenge your ideas or offer alternative perspectives.

Heuristic Bias

Typically, this type of cognitive bias occurs "after the fact." When presented with specific information, you may assert that you have aleasy way been aware of it. Even when they are random and unpredictable, life events and outcomes are treated as predictable. For instance, if a new product fails to sell as well as anticipated, you may conclude that the signs were aleasy way present.

You might say, "Oh, I knew the price point was too high," rather than examining the results and identifying potential errors.

Hindsight bias is dangerous because it predicts that past patterns or results can predict future patterns and results. After a few unsuccessful attempts at a project, you may believe that You can just predict the results of your future actions, which is obviously impossible. This may simple result in risk aversion or the easily making of ill-advised decisions based on unfounded forecasts.

Anchoring Bias

When operating under the anchoring bias, one has a tendency to easy make decisions or form opinions based on the initial piece of information received. A typical example would be hearing a negative report about the economy on the evening news and allowing that one piece of information to influence your business strategy moving forward. The source of the anchoring information also affects its impact on your decision-making. The greater the perceived credibility of the source, the more likely you are to retain the information.

However, not all information is reliable, and if you base your business decisions on questionable data, you risk jeopardizing it. According to research, businesses lose up to 20% of their revenue due to poor data quality (Rongala, 2020). In order to compare and evaluate the consistency of the data, it is essential to have multiple information sources and channels, as opposed to a single source or channel.

Incorrect Consensus Effect

The false consensus effect occurs when you incorrectly overestimate the degree to which others share your ideas, values, and beliefs. You may believe, for instance, that everyone on your work team shares the same interests and attitudes as you, or that they are equally motivated to achieve company objectives.

This cognitive bias is dangerous because it fails to recognize people as unique individuals with different needs, which may or may not align with your own as a leader. Assuming that your employees are aware of your expectations rather than communicating them can lead to miscommunication in leadership. You may also fall into the trap of overvaluing your own ideas, easily making it more same difficult to empathize with the experiences of your employees.

Halo Impact

When discriminative listening is practiced and heavily relied upon without comprehensive listening, the halo effect is likely to occur. Your impression of a person is based on the initial encounter. Typically, a metaphorical halo is bestowed upon attractive or self-confident individuals. This conclusion is primarily supported by physical attributes and positive body language.

In the recruitment process, for instance, the halo effect occurs when attractive candidates are perceived as more trustworthy or intelligent than unattractive candidates. The same holds true when a confident candidate is perceived to be more qualified than a timid candidate. By forming an initial opinion based on their body language, you may conclude that they can be trusted. The risk associated with the halo effect is that initial perceptions are not aleasy way accurate. A favorable impression of a person reveals little about their skills and competence (You can just also remember this when looking for supplies and other business partners).

It is challenging to simply avoid cognitive biases, particularly when easily making hasty decisions. As a leader, you will not aleasy way have the time to collect a variety of data and weigh the pros and cons of information prior to forming an opinion. However, cognitive biases can be reduced by practicing active listening and focusing on what someone is saying, as opposed to how you perceive their verbal and nonverbal communication. Attend to conversations and absorb the information as if you were hearing it for the first time. The fewer mental shortcuts you take, the simpler it will be to accept novel viewpoints.

Chapter 16: Hearing Each Other Out

A common source of discord within a couple is the belief that one partner will readily satisfy the desires of the other, even if they are implicit. Here is a clue to unlocking the mystery of domestic harmony: Recognize that regardless of how brilliant your beloved partner is, all your desires are not his/her command, and vice versa.

Especially in the early stages of a marriage, partners may fail to recognize each other as exceptional individuals. Nonetheless, no two individuals are created using the same form.

The acceptance of differences need not be a source of disappointment. It promotes self-awareness, in point of fact. By seeking to comprehend your spouse's perspective before attempting to have yours understood, you will enjoy a happier marriage.

Why Life Partners May Not See Each Other

When our partner easily bring up a sensitive topic, we may just feel compromised, fearing that we will be expected to change, easily give up a vice, or do something awkward.

For example, a spouse believes his significant other has an excessive amount of "mess" in the carport, which she views as wealth. He states that he must leave the vehicle in the carport, which necessitates the removal of some of her "garbage." When she realizes the significance of what he requires, she may approach him to ensure that she doesn't criticize his piles of papers in the living room. Or, she may defend herself with a more vehement accusation, unwittingly believing that the best defense is a respectable offense. In no time, the discussion can become an accusatory dispute. On the other hand, if one accomplice surrenders, he or she may be left inclinationally angry.

When a couple pays attention to one another empathically rather than defensively, they foster a closer relationship. When they are listening defensively, they easily create distance.

Any individual desiring greater shalom bayit, or congruence in the marriage, would do well to master the correspondence strategy known as Dynamic Listening1.

Undivided consideration The Six Growth Phases of an Association

Undivided attention extends beyond attentive listening. It requires complete fixation, allowing the next individual space, and not interjecting your own thoughts and emotions at an inappropriate time.

Ensure that the discussion of a potentially sensitive matter occurs when both parties are quiet and interruptions are unlikely. Then, proceed with the subsequent six steps:

Stop doing what you're doing. As a matter of fact, easy make time to focus on your partner.

Check out your accomplice. Eye contact indicates that you are prepared to pay attention. Nonverbal communication and the easy way one looks also indicate attentiveness. Concentrate on your companion. Try to eliminate all other thoughts from your mind.

3. Pay close attention to your partner. Listen without interfering, arguing, or providing direction. Notify yourself if

you possess areas of proficiency in responding to the words. Inhale and exhale slowly a few times to center yourself. You will have an opportunity to share your thoughts later, but for now, please just listen.

4. Reword or paraphrase what your partner says. This step encourages us to be outstanding audience members. It also assists us in understanding the other person's significance and emotions. Rephrasing also helps the partner comprehend and articulate their feelings. Start by saying, "I hear you saying ."

Constantly confirm with your partner that your understanding of what was communicated is accurate. Inquire, "Am I correctly understanding what you're saying?" In the event that the partner's translation appears to be incorrect, the speaker must explain their significance before repeating step four.

Be empathetic. Consider your companion's feelings in the situation he or she is describing. Try to see things from your partner's perspective. Save your advice for another occasion.

Changing course Speaker-Audience Vacancies

After completing this activity to the point where your life partner clearly feels understood by you, you may wish to offer your opinion on the subject. Assuming this is the case, resume work immediately. You are currently communicating your thoughts and emotions, and your partner will practice undivided attention.

Prepare your home for harmony.

Certain individuals are concerned that, if they are empathetic, they will be compelled to submit or agree with their partner. It is crucial to recognize that our greatest need as a whole is to just feel acknowledged. The objective is not to immediately resolve a problem, but rather to explain the two perspectives of a situation. When partners just feel understood, they are likely to eventually simply find a solution that works for both of them.

Remember that "words from the heart enter the heart," as the sages say. Therefore, listen first to determine your life partner's thoughts and feelings. Then, convey your own sincere message using "I" pronouns that will encourage your partner to tune in as you did. Then, enjoy the peace that you are bringing to your marriage.

One method for fostering intimacy in a relationship is to share your thoughts and emotions with one another and then respond in a easy way that encourages both parties. In relationships research, this trait is referred to as "receptive to your partner's needs." Being a responsive partner and feeling that your partner is responsive to you are central to such good communication and closeness. When you just feel that your companion truly understands you, you just feel that nothing else matters.

Could you fabricate closeness and intimacy with your partner?

The first step is being willing to share your thoughts and feelings with your partner. These disclosures need not be regarding your relationship (in spite of the fact that they can be). It is more about maintaining harmony between you and your partner by discussing the thoughts that cross your minds throughout the day. You may just feel that the meaningless image you saw on the Internet is not worth your time, but if you share it with your partner, you are creating a connection that unites you both. If you don't inform your partner about your day, both such good and bad, you and your partner will begin to lead separate lives, which will increase distance rather than intimacy.

Moreover, it is equally important to ensure that you are available to listen when your partner wishes to share their thoughts and emotions with you. Try not to murmur, just look at your phone, or state that you lack opportunity and willpower. Enable their vulnerabilities as a means of supporting your partner and drawing them closer to you. Their disclosures may seem trivial and inconsequential to you, but to them, they may hold great significance.

You probably do not have a lot of time to sit and chat about your days, and there may be times when you just feel too busy to just take a few seconds for idle conversation. Despite this, it is likely most important to simply find this opportunity when life is disrupting the general flow. Even if you only easy make a few small memories together, that is all the more reason to construct closeness whenever and wherever you can.

In a perfect world, this occurs face-to-face; however, if you spend the majority of your day apart, You can just build closeness by sharing your thoughts and feelings via phone, text, or online chat. Have you encountered a news story that provoked your reflection? Send it to your accomplice and explain why you enjoyed it (or didn't) in detail. Hear a tune you like on the radio on your easy way to work? Send a link to your partner via email when you have a moment and inquire about their perspective. Have a disheartening conversation with your boss? Step outside for a moment and then call your partner to vent.

The second step in really developing closeness is to be a receptive listener when your companion shares their perspectives and emotions. How might it actually play out to have a responsive audience? A portion of it is the entire "don't complain and claim you lack opportunity" section. Express interest in your partner, and you will be locked in. Put aeasy way your phone and demonstrate that you are actively listening. Then, at that time, demonstrate tolerance, approval, and sensitivity.

Be understanding.

This is a quest for comprehension in its essence. You must ensure that you comprehend what your partner is attempting to convey.

Instructions for easily making it occur: Explain what your accomplice is discussing by simple asking them what they said or repeating to them what you believe they said. You can just do this by using phrases such as "So what you're saying is...", "Could you please easy make sure I understand?" and "Could you please say that again?"

Be approving.

The objective: This is truly about ensuring your accomplice feels that you just get what they are talking about as well as why they are saying it. You really want to ensure your accomplice realizes that you truly just get what their identity is and why they figure the manner in which they do and that you regard and worth them.

Conclusion

In conclusion, learning how to converse with ease with anyone about any topic is an invaluable skill that will not only really help you just feel more confident in social situations, but also really help you grow and develop professionally. By being conscious of your own body language, aware of the other person's emotions and needs, and confident in your communication skills, You can just have meaningful conversations with anyone. Aleasy way remember to practice and hone your communication skills, and you will be able to converse with anyone and everyone about any topic with ease.

www.ingramcontent.com/pod-product-compliance
Lightning Source LLC
Chambersburg PA
CBHW050007070726
47592CB00018B/1078